HOW TO
Bounce
Back
FROM
LIFE'S
SETBACKS
The Family Way

How To Bounce Back
From Life's Setbacks

The Family Way

Compiled by

Dr. Tabatha M. W. Spurlock

**Dr. Shawnrell Blackwell • Deitra Wynn Scott • Lorene G. Williams
And Other Contributing Authors**

Empower One, Inspire Many LLC

As the visionary author, I dedicate this book to my beautiful daughter, Kennedi Alyse, and the children of my fellow co-authors. You all are the reasons we work so hard, dream so big, and love you more than we can put into words at times. You may not understand some decisions we make, but know that we have your best interests at heart. No matter where life takes you, know that you are deeply cherished and endlessly supported.

Table of Contents

Introduction

When life gets hard, it's challenging to understand how you will bounce back from your toughest setbacks in the moment. Whether you're facing financial hardship, loss, illness, or even conflict, bouncing back "the family way" includes love, unity, and shared hope. The latter requires open communication, mutual support, and faith as you heal and grow stronger. Setbacks help build character and can deepen bonds while inspiring perseverance. Every challenge presents an opportunity to rediscover your strength within and potentially new beginnings.

At the onset of this project, I was in the midst of a new beginning (i.e. legal separation and pending divorce). In the beginning, I thought it would be a great idea to tell the story of how my ex and I were effective at the ebbs and flows of co-parenting. I wanted to inspire other parents going through a similar journey and experience to not conform to what society will tell us or make us believe we have to endure...the bickering, fighting, knock out arguments, emotionally and financially draining court hearings, and dreadful exchanges at drop off/pick up. I've witnessed many

Introduction

of those firsthand as a bonus mother to two others between two long-term relationships. They were no fun to experience and the children were the ones who ended up hurt and caught in the middle.

On the other hand, I was excited to talk about the memories of my late great grandfather, Mr. Bobbie Dudley, and how I wanted to relive childhood moments as a source of hope and inspiration to bring my family and other families back together. As I began to promote the book, I connected with some amazing co-authors who had a strong desire to tell their stories of transformation and family empowerment. Stories of "coming out" to their family and friends, life post divorce, educating and empowering our kids in a questionable society, the power of prayer, recovering from health and physical setbacks, and how we as parents strive to raise productive citizens in society.

As you read our book, feel free to take notes at the end of each chapter on ways your family can grow closer or acknowledge what's currently helping your family thrive. It's also important to acknowledge that family may not always be blood so don't overlook key people in your village who show up when you need them. The goal of the book is to bring families closer together as we are transparent and authentic with how we too have bounced back from life's setbacks.

Back to the Basics

Dr. Tabatha Spurlock

D o you recall family gatherings as a child with your cousins and other relatives? Did anyone else enjoy holidays and time out of school when family members from out of town would come and stay at your house? There weren't enough bedrooms or beds for everyone, but you didn't care. You simply made "pallets" on the floor with blankets, sheets, and pillows. You were humble and full of love, regardless of the circumstances. Do those questions bring back any warm and fuzzy childhood memories? They certainly do for me!

I was raised in Chester, Virginia by a single mother as the eldest of three in a disadvantaged community also known as "The Hood!" Since my mom loved to cook and entertain guests, my family would always visit our home to stay while in town, especially for Thanksgiving and the Fourth of July. My grandmother lived in the country and her brothers—except for my Uncle Bill, who was in Petersburg—would bring their families from Baltimore and Philadelphia to visit. Her sister, who migrated to New York, would bring her family down as well. Everyone would visit Virginia primarily to see my great grandfather, Bobbie Dudley AKA Papa. They brought their children so that we could get to know each other, build bonds, and have a good southern time. We didn't need a big house. We just needed each other and the genuine love that exuded in the rooms while together. We would laugh for hours, bake silly cakes, play outside, and create lasting memories in our 3-bedroom apartment that was full of love.

Growth.

In 2024, I became a visionary author for the first time. I co-authored several books in recent years, telling pieces of my story until I finally had the courage to recruit authors as a self-publisher. The book ended up becoming a #1 New Release and #1 Best-Seller on Amazon. I didn't do it alone, though. I invested in coaches, vendors, and other visionary authors to understand the publishing process to one day be in a position to expand my business. The book was titled *"How to Bounce Back from Life's Setbacks"* and I said "Wow, this book is really resonating with people." I used that phrase as a title in another book and spoke it over and over throughout my accident recovery. As I started to think about my next book, I decided to keep the same theme and produce a sequel, adding the words "The Family Way" as I reflected on family values and norms that had dissipated over the years.

As I look at my family's current status and talk with friends about theirs, it hits me hard that something significant is missing in today's society. While I know there are families who come together often and are close, my family didn't have that anymore. What happened to the years of holiday gatherings with relatives from out-of-town spending the night? What happened to the frequent family outings? Short answer...death and grief! The great grandparents, grandparents, great uncles and great aunts from The Greatest Generation to Baby Boomers were gone, and the remaining generations were challenged with keeping traditions alive. With my Dudley family, there were a few attempts over the years that eventually fell flat. With my Spurlock family, it was a different story.

Grief.

Our lives began to drastically shift after the passing of my brother-in-law, father-in-law, stepfather, and mother-in-law, respectively, in a period of 20 months. The family gatherings were few and far between because the family dynamics shifted and the remaining members weren't in an amicable space. My healing process for grieving was delayed as I tried to be there for everyone else. As I've always done as the eldest, I put my feelings on a shelf. Deep inside, I was hurting too, and I felt like no one cared. I was masterful in showing up every day in every space like this person who had it all together and everything figured out. What else was I supposed to do? Show up broken and hurt? Expose my depression that was triggered by the grief after years of healing? By that time, my anxiety and depression had elevated to a highly functional state. Today, I realize I could've been more vulnerable over the years with my raw feelings versus trying to be the "strong person" all the time. It was a natural trauma response.

As the eldest sibling, I matured early on for my age. As a result, I've received a lot of praise from people who have admired my strength and how I have taken the lead with past situations. I checked off all the life boxes that were presented to me only to be left feeling as if I didn't allow space or time to determine which boxes I wanted for my own life. The pressure was heavy many times, and I had to learn how to figure it out without looking like a failure. Failure wasn't an option until it was the only thing on the table. What people didn't know was that I was in survival mode carrying around burdens, meeting others' needs while neglecting my own as a wife and mother, managing chaos and a household, and not knowing how to effectively communicate (as an over communicator) my needs to others and how to ask for help.

As an adult, I can now process my resilience and strength from a different lens. I'm constantly reminded that my help comes from the Lord because it must have been Him in the trenches with me through many of the battles I've fought and still fight. The extended grace and love in the midst of hurt at times and questioning how I survived what was meant to break me. The need for softness, safety, and spaces where I didn't have to be so resilient all the time just didn't seem like they were in the cards for me. I was a leader who was reliable, punctual, an overachiever, and successful at most tasks. As a result, the invitations to serve and lead in various capacities would be extended. As I was serving, I ultimately wanted to build a life for my daughter in a world that didn't exist during my childhood.

Adulthood.

During my childhood, we did our best to navigate through every socioeconomic factor plaguing our neighborhood and lifestyle. As I matriculated through college and began to explore the world, I learned about networking and social organizations that were full of individuals who supported and helped others navigate through life together and at an easier pace. It was an extended family that one could inherit through membership and service from organization to organization. While over time I started to reach a state of burnout, I was beginning to question time spent and whether I really capitalized on the very thing I initially sought out, which was extended family and friendships. Imposter syndrome from my childhood had me believing that I didn't belong in the very spaces I earned a spot. The juggle of the life I was in pursuit of and the one that I inherited when I became a wife felt at times like two different worlds struggling to merge. Unfortunately, a spiritual foundation was missing. While the Lord and His word and church were a part of our lives, there wasn't a familial commitment necessary to help keep the family unit together with much needed support.

When I initially thought of the topic and focus of this book, I was in a space of marital separation. I didn't discuss it publicly, but it was happening in real time. As I navigated this new normal after almost 20 years with over 18 years of marriage, I wanted to leave a legacy for my daughter and to share with others an effective approach to co-parenting. I was also missing my family. For those who know me, I've always been a family person. I have always been the nucleus of getting people together to gather for holidays, birthdays, anniversaries, Sunday football, and any other occasion that I felt justified having people together. I clearly inherited that giving spirit from my mother. Having a family of my own, even in the midst of an unraveling marriage, was a big part of the reason I tried to hang on and figure out how to make it work. But I was losing a battle that was bigger than me. And to be honest, my tough exterior was likely sending the wrong message while my heart was too big and still available through the pain. My faith was wavering, and I became consumed with going through the motions day to day and year to year to make sense of my life as a divorced and co-parenting mother.

Life Happens.

From house to house, the moves began to be overwhelming. I was going through the motions, trying to put a life plan together piece by piece while the pieces were falling apart. On the outside, I had it all together. I was taking care of home, excelling at work, showing up at meetings and social gatherings, and making our daughter's academics a priority. However, on the inside, I was having an emotional breakdown and struggled to find my way and an outlet. I didn't want to expose what I was really experiencing and left my overall thoughts and feelings of the demise of my marriage in the counseling sessions over the years and with those family and friends whom I thought I could trust. I did my best to protect myself, our family image, and our professional statuses from the opinions of others who were quick to pick a side based upon popularity or those who jumped on a "I just don't like her" bandwagon without really having a reason to dislike me. The strength I thought I displayed came from a place of not speaking publicly about my personal life because it was none of anyone's business and I didn't want to hinder God's promises and favor over my life. However, my silence began to take a silent toll on me emotionally, mentally, and physically because it began to feel heavy and I was feeling empty inside due to isolating myself from others.

After years of discussing healing and bouncing back, this time I thought I was doing better by going deeper with a few trusted people in my village and being vulnerable about how I was really feeling. However, it took time pulling back the layers because I didn't trust myself completely to say to the people who had held me in such high regard and expected me to win in life that "I messed up!" I didn't mess up by leaving my marriage because I ultimately felt like we reached a point where both of our needs weren't getting met as a couple. I loved someone with every ounce of my being and felt forced to walk away to save myself from the physical, emotional, and mental toll it was taking on me. However, my hope was that we could have an amicable co-parenting relationship as still family and friends.

Instead of seeking love and support from those I held in high regard, I should've gone back to therapy. I should've found a professional to help me work through my feelings and not keep unresolved feelings built up for so long. I should've joined a ministry at church sooner for spiritual connection. The publicity of my life, partly due to my outgoing personality, was taking a toll on how I showed up for myself because people expected to see the jovial, outgoing person I initially became and not the adult who was finally processing childhood trauma and needed a certain kind of love that she was afraid to ask for. The woman who poured so much into a relationship for the majority of her adult life to now navigating life as a single woman with a child was a process. The overthinker was trying to figure it out alone and stand on business in some areas while the battles were slowly being lost.

As I tried to find my way, not necessarily as a woman, but more so as a mother, I was reminded of my childhood memories. I began to question, "What were those things that brought me joy as a child?" It wasn't a parent who was struggling to make ends meet by working multiple jobs. I admired and inherited my mother's hustling spirit and grind. However, with this current generation and times as a parent, that way of living was becoming ineffective and mundane. I began to yearn for a life that required less masculine energy of having it all together to one embracing softness where I performed less and allowed others to show up for me where needed. This new approach would allow me to be a better person who felt more present in the moments of life versus the planner who had it all figured out from a success standpoint.

Again, I checked off all the life boxes that were expected of me as a child and adult in order. Now what? After watching the movie "The Life List," I devoted time to creating my own life list of boxes to check off. The anxiety I inherited over the years, as a high achieving woman, was a trauma response from growing up as the "good girl" who didn't make mistakes, had it all figured out, and walked on eggshells with others trying to be perfect for acceptance and love. As I struggled to figure things out, I made a few costly mistakes that were atypical. My trauma was starting to become my identity. I was worrying when I should've been worshipping. I was showing up in the building regularly and kept a song in my heart and could get to a scripture if and when needed; however, I still lacked focus and clarity with my new walk.

Typically, the one who gives a lot is one who also likes to receive a lot and won't communicate it because it comes across like begging or seeking attention, as if that's a bad thing. I love and I loved hard...I'm guilty. And it took years for me to realize that I was losing myself and my self-worth. I lost sight of my value while I was able to coach others in realizing theirs. It didn't make me ineffective at my craft as a coach, but it did make me question my own life and its purpose.

Conclusion.

To the parent out there trying to figure it out too, I extend to you the following affirmations - (say it aloud):

"It's ok to have a good heart. I'm not perfect and I give myself permission to release the strongholds of false expectations for me and how I show up for others. As I heal, I understand and am accepting of what happened to me. I won't become a hurt person who hurts others. I know better and will do better. Boundaries are healthy and help me protect my peace and enforce self-respect. I will find a way to turn my pain into purpose. I will restore what was stolen and heal what was broken. I will find the inner and external strength to walk like the victory has already been won."

For those who continue to engage in family traditions to keep the love flowing, I commend you. For those who are integrating new traditions, I commend you. To those who don't have either; however, you have been inspired to start today, I commend you and hope your family is able to bounce back from life's setbacks the family way!

Meet the Visionary Author | Dr. Tabatha Spurlock

Dr. Tabatha Spurlock is a dynamic and highly energetic motivational speaker, life coach, best-selling author, and educator. For 20+ years, she has been committed to youth from the Boys & Girls Club to the public K-12 education system. In her current capacity, she helps foster community partnerships and promotes career pathways while being heavily involved in philanthropic efforts as a member of several nonprofit organizations. As a native of Chester, Virginia, she proudly serves as a board member with the Chester YMCA.

In 2016, Dr. Spurlock was the victim of a traumatic accident that left her unable to walk unassisted for three months. In 2017, she founded a life empowerment company called Empower One, Inspire Many. She coaches clients on how to bounce back from life's setbacks with her "Like A B.O.S.S." coaching program. During the pandemic, she wrote a children's book titled "A Promise is a Promise" which focuses on resilience and displaying positive emotions in a negative situation. She designed a social-emotional learning (SEL) curriculum aligned with the book and has served as a guest author for elementary schools and after-school programs. Find out more at www.tabathaspurlock.com

NOTES

NOTES

NOTES

Held by the Village: A Journey Through Shadows and Strength

Deborah E. Goode

It was November 2006, one week before Thanksgiving. The sound of the moving truck hit harder than I expected. Today I'm not just packing boxes-I'm packing pieces of my life I thought would last. Saying goodbye to this home, and to the version of us that once lived here, broke my heart. It's the end of something I never imagined would end, and the start of something I never wanted to begin.

I remember calling my friend Cheryl. She was very encouraging as I cried, looking lost, saying "this can't be my life". But it was.

I recall trying to settle into my apartment. My sweet mother-in-law would come over and assist me with unpacking, lining every single cabinet shelf in my kitchen! I don't know if she knew it, but her presence was my peace.

The following week was Thanksgiving; my son Donavan and I stayed home. The weight of everything was too much, and I couldn't bear the smiles and small talk. But my son was my light. In the quiet, in the stillness, he reminded me of what love looks like, even in the hardest moments. He gave me strength when I felt like I had none.

December was heavy, Christmas was my favorite time of the year, full of joy, love, and togetherness. This year will be different. This year I faced the holidays as someone without a husband; without the family I once knew. The light felt dimmer, the silence louder.

My mom called me every day, just to check in, to hear my voice, to make sure I was holding on. She knew well what I was going through, so she knew the quiet kind of pain I was carrying. She hated seeing me suffer, but she never let me go through it alone. Her love held me up when everything else felt like it was falling apart.

My dad always reminded me to hold my head high. "Never let yourself go", he would say. Always look good, even when you are hurting inside. He taught me strength isn't about pretending everything is okay, it's about showing up with grace, even when it's difficult. His voice echoes in my mind on the toughest days, reminding me who I am.

I was blessed with the best in-laws in the world: supportive, kind, and loving.

As 2007 began, I made a quiet promise to myself, to take a year to simply be. To reflect, to feel, to break if needed to, and to heal at my own pace. I wanted to stop surviving and start being human again. No more pretending I was okay. Just honesty, growth, and the hope of rediscovering who I am beneath the pain.

In May 2007, the ball would begin to drop. My son's father would be placed on leave with pay for damaging allegations in the workplace. He was a federal employee. As he did every Memorial Day, he went to bike week in Myrtle Beach like he didn't have a problem in the world. When he returned, the ball completely dropped, he was placed on leave without pay. This would be a blow to both of us. *Jesus, can this get any worse?* Yes, it can and did!

In 2009, I sat in a federal courtroom. I remember looking at my son's father. His legs were shaking with fear. With our friend Gary and my brother-in-law Eric beside me, we were all in tears. This was unreal and would begin the next phase of my life. He was sentenced to 18 months in federal prison; my drive home was numb.

I carried on like everything was okay, even when I was breaking inside. I showed up day after day, because my son needed me. I put him first—always. He was a happy kid, full of light, even though I knew he missed his dad. His smile took my pain away.

2005-2009 were dark years. My son's father served exactly 12 months in federal prison. Nothing about it was easy. By the grace of God and my tribe, we made it!

My story does not end here. There are so many pieces to this puzzle.

To every mother, never give up on yourself. You are stronger than you know, your dreams matter. Children come first—your love, sacrifice, and presence shape their world. Keep pushing even on the hardest days.

I've always been a planner. I married my college sweetheart and dreamed of the house with the white picket fence, the life I thought I was building step by step. But God had other plans. Life didn't unfold the way I imagined, and that's been one of the hardest lessons to accept. Still, I'm learning to trust that even in the detours, there's purpose. Even in the loss, there's something waiting to be found.

Life isn't perfect, far from it. But somehow, I've never been happier. There's peace in accepting what is, joy in the little things, and strength in knowing I made it through. Happiness doesn't look like I once imagined, but it feels more real than ever. My son is now 25 years old, a member of Kappa Alpha Psi Fraternity and obtained his bachelor's degree in 2023. In December, he will graduate with his second degree. Upon graduation, he will be commissioned as a 2nd lieutenant for the US Army.

To my village, that I never formally thanked, this testament is for you! Thank you!! I've leaned on your love, support and strength more times than I can count. You've helped carry me through the hardest days and celebrated the joyful ones. You have been there for Donavan in ways I'll never forget. I am forever grateful.

The Village

- Ms. Hazel Edwards (mom)
- Mr. Charles Edwards (daddy)
- Mr. Donavan Goode (son)
- Mr. and Mrs. Edward Goode (bonus parents)
- Ms. Cheryl Williams
- Mr. Kevin Hall, Sr.
- Mr. and Mrs. Kem Goode
- Mr. Eric Goode
- Mr. Tracy Edwards
- Mr. Gary Martin
- Mr. and Mrs. Michael Davis
- Mr. Wayne Weaver (RIP)
- Gravel Hill Baptist Church family

Meet the Author | Deborah E. Goode

Deborah is a purpose-driven higher education professional with a strong foundation in relationship-building, alumni engagement, and philanthropic development. As Director of Development at Virginia Commonwealth University's School of Business, she leads strategic fundraising efforts and fosters meaningful connections between the university and its alumni, partners, and broader community.

When she's not building partnerships or championing education, you'll likely find her enjoying a good game, discovering a new winery, or planning her next travel adventure. Above all, she's most proud of her role as mother to her son, Donavan.

NOTES

NOTES

NOTES

Awakening the Matriarch: Heal Yourself, Empower Your Lineage

Anya Hildreth

S ociety will try to keep a woman suppressed, depressed, and oppressed. It will tell her to work harder, to ignore her intuition, to silence her voice, and to sacrifice her body in the name of productivity. But I have lived through this lie, and I know the cost. I was the woman who gave too much, who burned herself out trying to prove her worth in a world that never intended to honor it.

I was born into a world of privilege, the daughter of a black mother and a white father, raised overseas in a world of diplomatic immunity, maids, chauffeurs, and gated compounds. My life was one of comfort, adventure, and freedom. I was the child of diplomats, shielded from the harsh realities of racism and sexism, living in a world where my American passport carried weight and my family's status commanded respect.

But when I moved back to the United States at 17, the privilege I had known was stripped away. I quickly learned that here, privilege was a different currency — one based on the color of your skin, your proximity to whiteness, and your willingness to play by the rules of a patriarchal society. I had been raised to stand out, but suddenly, I was expected to blend in.

I pushed through college, landed a full-time job in business development, and then taught myself how to become an engineer when someone told me I had the mind for it. I became a single mom seven years into my career, learning to balance the demands of motherhood with the high expectations of corporate life. For over a decade, I hustled, grinding through 60-hour workweeks, co-parenting two kids, and doing the work of two people in a male-dominated industry. I received awards, promotions, and high performance reviews, but the cost was high.

I was asked to take notes in meetings while my male peers contributed ideas. I was asked to order lunch for the team while balancing engineering projects, audits, and leading diversity groups. I was the workhorse — the go-to person, the one who never said no.

Then came the physical collapse. Hashimoto's. Type 1 diabetes. My body literally started to eat itself. I ignored the early signs — the fatigue, the weight loss, the brain fog — until it was too late. I kept pushing, kept grinding, kept trying to prove my worth, until my body forced me to stop.

Imagine being an engineer suddenly thrown into a warehouse to pull a '4 car load' — loading a mound of packages into four different vehicles before 9:30 am. We arrived at midnight, and the shifts never seemed to end. All of us — engineers, sales, HR, finance, and marketing — were in the trenches together, all hands on deck.

I had been an athlete my whole life, a former CrossFitter when my kids were little, and I knew what hard work felt like. But this was different.

My body started to break down. I got slower, my mind struggled to remember where the packages were supposed to go, and I felt my strength fading. I hadn't eaten because, by that point, I had been gluten-free for 8 years, and you can't just add gluten back into your body without suffering the consequences. I had been hospitalized twice for accidentally eating gluten — the intense stomach pain, the bloating, the feeling like my heart was about to explode.

With limited food options and barely any gluten-free choices, my body started to give out. I remember one supervisor finally finding enough Gatorade for us. I drank seven Gatorades back to back, desperate to replace the electrolytes I had sweated out. But something was wrong. I had just downed seven Gatorades, and I still felt empty.

Then came the on-road shift. We hopped into rental cars to deliver packages in an unfamiliar city. My vision started to blur. I couldn't see the numbers on the houses. My head felt heavy, and my heart raced uncontrollably. I became a driver helper the next day, and I remember falling asleep between every stop. I collapsed into my hotel bed that night and slept for 24 hours straight after just three days of this grind.

When I finally made it home, I dragged myself to the doctor. My A1C was 12. I was in DKA (Diabetic Ketoacidosis), dangerously close to being admitted. I was given a stack of prescriptions and a grim look from my doctor, who told me my life had just changed forever.

But I refused to be controlled by a cocktail of drugs. I went home and tried to revive my pancreas the only way I knew how — clean, natural food, relentless discipline, and a complete overhaul of my lifestyle. I cut out sugar, alcohol, smoking, and processed junk. I connected with my spirituality and worked through my emotions.

I lost 35 pounds. I pushed my body to the edge to save what little pancreatic function I had left.

But a week later, my pancreas died. All my beta cells were gone. The organ that had kept me alive for decades finally gave up, and I was left with a mere 5% of its function. For the rest of my life, I would need to be connected to a pump or inject myself with insulin to survive.

I was devastated. But in that devastation, I found my purpose. I had no choice but to process it emotionally, mentally, spiritually, and physically. That rock-bottom moment became the foundation of my course, confirmed by years of research and interviews with over 100 women who had also hit their breaking points. It was the gift I never asked for, but the one that gave me the blueprint to not only save my own life but to empower others to save theirs.

And as a mother, I needed my children to see that healing is possible. That resilience is not about pretending to be strong—it's about learning how to rest, rise, and rebuild with grace. My kids witnessed my unraveling, but more importantly, they witnessed my return. And I want every woman to know: your healing sets the tone for your entire family.

I created my A.L.I.G.N. framework, the five of six pillars that guide my work:

Awaken Your Emotional Awareness—Release deep-seated emotional pain, heal trauma, and let go of the stories that no longer serve you.

Liberate Your Nervous System—Break free from chronic stress, regulate your body's responses, and find true peace.

Integrate Your Spiritual Essence—Reconnect with your higher self, trust your intuition, and find your purpose.

Ground Your Physical Health—Balance your hormones, stabilize your energy, and heal your body from the inside out.

Nurture Your Leadership and Boundaries—Reclaim your voice, own your power, and lead from a place of authentic alignment.

If you feel the call to break the cycle, to reclaim your power, and to become the matriarch your lineage deserves, let's walk this path together. Heal yourself, and you heal those who come after you. This isn't just about you — it's about the generations that will follow in your footsteps.

Awaken the matriarch within you. Heal yourself. Empower your lineage.

Meet the Author | Anya Hildreth—Holistic Life Coach & Generational Healer

Anya Hildreth is a former corporate engineer turned holistic life coach and spiritual powerhouse for women who do it all but feel empty inside. After spending years climbing ladders in a world that never truly saw her, Anya hit a breaking point—diagnosed with Type 1 diabetes at the height of stress and self-sacrifice. But rock bottom became her turning point.

Now, she blends science and soul, helping high-achieving women regulate their nervous systems, break ancestral cycles, and reclaim their feminine power. Through her signature A.L.I.G.N.™ Framework and Soul Work method, she leads women to reconnect with their true selves—emotionally, spiritually, and physically.

She is also a proud mother of two, whose journey toward wholeness was deeply inspired by and for her children.

If you're ready to stop performing and start becoming, Anya is here to help you rise. Because healing yourself is healing your lineage.

Citizens of Life Integrative Wellness

NOTES

NOTES

NOTES

Testimony of Faith

Lorene G. Williams

Hello, my name is Lorene Williams and I'm a woman of faith with an overwhelming belief in the power of prayer. I gave my life to God at the age of nine in the year of our Lord 1971.

I'm the granddaughter of Bobbie and Sallie Dudley, who raised me in a Baptist upbringing. My grandmother had a love for God that many felt ashamed of. Some even feared because in those days when you expressed your love for God, people looked at you differently.

The Holy Spirit would come over her on Sunday morning in service and her hat would fly one way and her purse another. Grandma talked about God every, and I mean, everywhere she went. Sadly, my grandma passed in 1973.

Now my grandfather, who was called Papa, Daddy, and Bobbie to those that knew him, was my heart. He was a deacon in church and a true man of God. He was a man of few words. Meek and humble all the time. When he spoke, we listened, and he only had to speak to us once. On Sunday, when it was his turn to pray, there was a threshold in the atmosphere. As a young girl, I wasn't aware that it was the Anointing of the Holy Spirit. Although I knew I welcomed his prayers. Papa left this world in February 1997. I remember getting ready to go out the door to the funeral and I stopped and told my family... daddy prayed hard for us. Now we have to pray for ourselves.

At the time, I wasn't sure of how to pray. Though I knew I had to learn to pray for my children and myself. I give all honor and glory to God because He taught me how to pray.

Easter Sunday 2010, I had visited a friend's church after her and I read scripture and prayed eight hours the day before. At the time of Alter Call, I went to the front of the church for prayer. There were four people, including myself. When the pastor came to me last; he asked me what was my petition for prayer. Previously, I would always ask for the prayer of peace, but this time, for the first time, I asked for the gift of speaking in tongues. At that very moment, the pastor laid his hand on my stomach and uttered these words: Out of your belly flow living waters. Right there, right then, God blessed me with the gift of the Holy Spirit.

2025 is my 15th Anniversary as well as my 15th year of praying on social media. Whether there was one person or more, I have always relied on God to speak to my spirit and guide me as to what to say. Often times when I look back over the prayers, I can't believe they were written by me. I'm in awe of God in how He allows me to do this assignment for Him.

Whether praying on post, over the phone, or holding someone's hand in agreement, I want to glorify God in this journey called life.

You see, I'm not ashamed of the Gospel of Jesus Christ. I'm not perfect nor do I try to be, but I have always had this motto to my life... *"I would rather serve God and there not be a God than to not serve God and there is. For God is whom I fear."*

Being called to do God's will is not easy. My best conversations are when I'm talking about God with another brother or sister. For no matter what's going on in life, God can turn every situation around. Not because we're worthy, but because He's merciful.

June 2023, I had a heart attack and was diagnosed with stage 2 cancer. There were days when my body was so sick that I could be hungry and not have the strength to make it out of bed. Days where I waited to be with my Lord on the other side of Glory. You see, that was not my portion. Though the journey has been difficult, God still carried me through.

Nearly a year ago, in April 2024, God spoke to me sitting on my daughter's porch. Suddenly He said I gave you the gift, but you're not using it. You see, the prayers and poems that I have prayed and written throughout the years were for the track record of who lives in me. God gave me the assignment of Prayer Frames. Wow, at that moment, the Anointing was so powerful that I called a friend and told her what God had spoken to me. My body was trembling, and I was crying to the point I could barely get the words out. I mean, the Holy Spirit was all over me. It was a Divine feeling and one that I'm still in awe of.

When I told another friend about the experience, she sowed seed to get the frames started, and then life happened and the dream and vision were delayed.

Never delay an assignment from God because night and day my spirit is moved with the how's, why's, when's, and where's. *Lord, how am I going to do this? What door will open for the masses to be reached?*

Well... you know the God we serve that sits high and looks low....
He never ceases to amaze me. I titled my prayers years ago, *Holy
Spirit Speak*. To God be the glory. The vision God laid in my spirit
is now *Holy Spirit Speak, LLC*. The goals are the Prayer Frames,
T-shirts, Mugs, and Tumblers. Every item has a prayer embedded
in them.

You see, I never knew the prayers Daddy prayed over me and the
mission God gave me years ago would be for this purpose. I'm
trusting God to touch hearts to stand in agreement with me as we
bind in unity for the Holy Spirit to lead, guide, and direct us to be
pleasing in God's sight.

I'm humbled, honored, and filled with gratitude for such a task as
this to reach my brothers and sisters across the world. I speak life
over these prayers and I don't doubt the Trinity to touch souls with
love, peace, joy, prosperity, forgiveness, compassion, strength,
fortitude, faith, grace, and mercy.

For faith is the substance of things hoped for, although those things
aren't seen. As I go through this journey called life, I will strive to
do God's will. My love for God is unmeasured, and my anointing
is priceless.

As I pray and produce the *Holy Spirit Speak LLC* items, I will
always give praise for the gift of being a prayer warrior for the
Kingdom of God.

As I end this narrative, I leave with prayers for my children,
grandchildren, family, and friends. May God continue to smile
down with grace and mercy.

Daughter's Prayer

Father God, thank you for my daughter/daughters. Thank You for allowing me the gift of being their mother. Thank You for allowing me to watch them grow from infancy to princess, to queens.

Father God, I ask that You encamp Your Warring Angels around them every second, every minute, and every hour of the day.

Touch them, Father God, from the crown of their head to the soles of their feet. Bless them, Father God, with strength and endurance for any obstacles that may come their way.

Rain over them, Father God, with a fresh anointing that lets them acknowledge You as their Lord and Savior.

Bless them, Father God, with a loving and forgiving heart. Protect them, Father God, from all hurt, harm, and danger that is not of You.

Bless them, Father God, to be in plenty and not in want. Humble them, Father God, to put their trust in You. Touch them, Father God, to be pleasing in Your sight.

In Jesus Christ Blessed Name I Pray. Amen.

Son's Prayer

Most gracious and loving Father God, thank You for my son/sons. Lord, I thank You for allowing me to nurture him from a baby to a boy and a man.

Thank You, Father God, for such a precious gift as being his mother. Thank You for the tools that You gave me to watch him be kind to mankind.

Thank You for empathy and compassion. Thank You for blessing him with strength, fortitude, and endurance to embrace the vicissitudes of life.

Father God, I ask that You keep a circle around him. Touch him, Father God, in a mighty way that only You can provide.

Bless him, Father God, with love, peace, joy, and prosperity. Give him what he may stand in need of to be the best man that he can be.

Forgive him, Father God, if he has wronged anyone and let not his heart be troubled by anyone or anything.

In Jesus Christ Blessed Name I Pray. Amen

Grandchildren's Prayer

Father God, thank You. Thank You for my/our grandchildren. I thank You for allowing me to see another generation of our bloodline. I thank You for the joy these precious children bring.

I thank You, Father God, for a long life to watch them grow and become men and women of God, just like their ancestors.

I ask Father God that You will touch them from the oldest to the youngest with the wisdom and knowledge they need to be successful in this journey called life.

I ask Father God that You encamp Your Warring Angels around them to keep them from hurt, harm, and danger. Bless them Father God.

As they go about their day, Father God, I ask that they have a spirit of kindness and that that kindness is returned to them. Remove anybody or anything that means them no good thing.

Touch them, Father God. Your right hand allows their paths to be blessed and anointed by You. Give them, Father God, focus, clarity, wisdom, and knowledge to excel.

Bless them, Father God, with a spirit of love, peace, joy, prosperity, grace, and mercy.

In Jesus Christ Blessed Name I Pray. Amen.

Family Prayer

Father God, thank You for family. Thank You for my brothers and sister that You allowed to be called family.

Thank You, Father God, for those I accept as family though our bloodline may-not be the same. Father God, thank You for the blessing that people have been to us with their joy and laughter.

Thank You for the blessing of having a listening ear and a shoulder to cry on.

Thank You for family that had a heart for mankind. Thank You for the good and bad times because You taught us to love harder.

Father God, I ask that You bless us to continue to love one another despite what things look like. Bless us, Father God, to be a blessing because life could've been another way.

Bless our bloodline, Father God, to forever love and respect one another. Bless us all, Father God, with longevity in life in our bodies and please touch us with a replenishing anointing of supernatural healing from above.

In Jesus Christ Blessed Name I Pray. Amen.

Meet the Author | Lorene Williams

Lorene Williams is a senior with a deep passion for prayer. Her unwavering faith in the power of prayer gives her strength and courage through life's journey. She recently founded Holy Spirit Speak LLC, a business inspired by her belief that prayer is the key to unlocking every situation. They offer Prayer Frames, T-shirts, Mugs, and Tumblers—all designed to carry and display powerful prayers in our daily lives. She believes words hold power, and there is no weapon more effective or empowering than the spoken word of prayer. Prayer changes everything.

NOTES

NOTES

NOTES

Our Aunt America Needs Us

Deitra Wynn Scott

We sit down to dinner and my 6-year-old daughter leads us in grace. "Thank you, God, for this food and for my family. Please bless all the people in the world. And... please don't let Donald Trump and Elon Musk take my mommy's job. Amen."

I didn't know whether to laugh or to cry. Our babies have come of political conversation age. At 12, 8, and now 7 and 7, they see what's happening in the world. They see the news, hear the President speak and spew, see the impact on people. They listen to us, they ask questions, they feel deeply. One of them said, "So he's saying we're too broke as a country to have *Meals on Wheels* and *Head Start*, but him and his friends only poop in gold toilets?"

Yeah, no, that's not the dream. Not the American Dream all our children deserve a shot at, that we raised them to believe could be any of ours. Their *Aunt America* raised them right alongside us just as she helped raise us. We wouldn't be who we are without her ratchet self. She does want *the Dream* for us, and we, the people, want our Aunt America to live up to her potential. And we got her back in it. Oh, she so promising!

47

She has a good heart (the people), strong bones (the Constitution), undeniable beauty (sea to shining sea), dazzling brains (infrastructure and innovation), and great taste (culture for days). But Auntie got some health problems. She could be treated and healed, yet the people in charge keep prescribing amputation. Nope, not having it. She's ours and we still believe in the very idea of America!

If we want to save our brilliant, beautiful, complicated matriarch over generations, we need to be honest with ourselves and our children about what's at stake for us and future generations, and how to be a family that fights together.

<u>This is a guide to help you teach your children to love, understand, and protect America.</u> Not blindly or just outwardly, but with fierce, caring action, powerful knowledge, and joy. This is about raising up little citizens America can count on, who will grow up to love their country by helping it do better. This is about how we save Aunt America, the family way.

PART ONE

Teach Them What Aunt America is Working With!

Auntie can get fly now! She has a whole governance structure, constitution, and history of greatness to build on. Let's talk about our assets. If we're Team Auntie, let's give our children some basic training on understanding her using team sports analogy.

Our Country Works Like a Team

The legislative branch: The team that writes the playbook - the laws. The executive branch: The coach calling the plays. The judicial branch: The refs making sure nobody's breaking the rules.

And behind the scenes, there's a whole support squad: position coaches (Department of Education), doctors and trainers (Health and Human Services), facilities management (Interior Department), and more. They keep things moving, clean, healthy, safe.

So, while the "big three" (legislative, executive, judicial) set the game in motion and call the shots, our forefathers were right in establishing these institutions with their expert staff who make sure the game actually runs efficiently, fairly, and for the benefit of the whole team (we, the people).

Walk them through how decisions are made, who has power, and why paying attention matters. The people behind the policies; what their jobs are, and why they need to be held accountable.

There's Levels to This: National, State, and Local Politics

If national politics is like setting rules for the whole sports league, state politics sets the rules for one team in that league. Local is closest to home, like your closest teammates you practice with who have the greatest influence on your game.

Every sports team has players and in the game of democracy, citizens are the players... that means you! Even if you're not old enough to vote yet, you're like a player-in-training or rookie on the bench learning the rules, practicing your skills, and getting ready to step on the field. You don't have to get ready if you stay ready! So, practice citizenship by speaking up, helping others, sharing your joy, and through teamwork.

Help Them Connect the Dots

Talk with your kids about how things work together and how things work in general. Microwaves, playgrounds, hospitals, countries, households. Everything it takes to keep them running smoothly. It'll help you appreciate others and appreciate the coordination, cooperation, and innovation.

Start with the food we eat and how it's grown and harvested by farmers and their staff, cleaned and possibly processed, transported, bought and sold by stores, with all these parts having safety and regulation policies to be met before being bought and prepared by us. When kids understand systems, they begin to see how things work and see what breaks when someone starts pulling pieces out.

Teach the Value of Our American Institutions

Aren't our American institutions part of what makes us great? What is our society like without them? Are we #1 if elderly and disabled people don't eat because they can't cook or go out, but Meals on Wheels was cancelled? Are we the best if kids start school already behind without Head Start? Are we patriotic when we don't provide the healthcare and support we promised veterans who risked their lives? Cancer research, Park Services, Social Security, funding to non-profits that are lifelines in society. These programs and institutions are not a waste. They make America great!

Global Citizenship

Be sure to remind them that America is just one of 190 countries on a planet full of wonderful people, places, and ideas. All the history, food, languages, music, and stories!

And we all want the same basic things: love, safety, family, and a good future. We trade with other countries. We solve big problems together (like climate change and peace). We learn from each other. And we help each other when there's a need. We're connected.

Teach Good Trouble in the Face of Tyranny

George Washington helped lead the fight for independence from a British king who had too much power, then became the first U.S. President. People trusted him so much he could have stayed in power forever, but he defied norms establishing that no one should have too much power, and America is led by laws, not rulers.

Harriet Tubman escaped from slavery and had the courage to go back again and again to help others escape too. Even though the law didn't live up to its promise that all people are created equal, she believed in God's higher law - that everyone deserves freedom, so she risked her life to help others find their way.

Cesar Chavez helped the farm workers who feed us get fair treatment and reminded America that the Constitution protects workers too, not just the powerful. He showed people how to unionize so they could have as much influence and power as the rich. His motto, "Yes, we can - together."

All our ancestors and forefathers, democracy titans or everyday people, real ones who fought for the full idea of America - the right to vote, to govern, to own land, to pursue happiness, to be innocent until proven guilty. The liberty to live. Teach them that being American means standing up for what's right. Not just when it's easy. Especially when it's not. Like John Lewis said, *Good Trouble*.

PART TWO

What We're Up Against

If we're really trying to protect Aunt America, we must be vigilant and account for the dangers she could face. Teach kids to watch for using God and religion to justify bigotry and oppression. Like saying Jesus wants prayer in schools, but not feeding the kids whose parents can't pay for lunch. Like saying abortion is wrong but letting people die without insulin.

Watch for consolidation of power that invalidates the checks and balances of the three co-equal branches. Follow the money, knowing outsized donations shift the power and accountability from the constituents to the donor. Watch for taking away voting rights so fewer people (targeted people) can have a say and participate in governing.

Mis- and disinformation are killing us! Purposefully dividing us. Learn to critically think about if something is true. Facts, opinions, or ads? Look things up together on trusted sources. Watch for hostility toward expertise, higher learning, and journalism, so there is no trusted source except one. Them.

These are all issues you can speak with your elected officials about and organize around.

PART THREE

It Starts at Home. Don't just talk about it. Live it.

Experiences! > Algorithms

No one knows your child's talents, interests, and needs better than you. Try to incorporate these into your lives, on special occasions, regularly, or day to day. Stimulate their minds and let them go deep into what interests them. It will build strong brain pathways in contrast to the screen's quick cuts that train the brain to expect constant stimulation with no time to think.

Hands-on, real-world experiences like visiting museums, parks, libraries, or learning skills don't just fill time, they build brains and shape hearts. When kids explore history, art, nature, or how things are made, they're not just learning facts, they're learning to ask questions, see connections, appreciate others, and contribute to the world around them.

Music, movies, or martial arts on YouTube, these experiences grow confidence, empathy, and agency... the roots of active, thoughtful citizenship. Practice debates over a family rule (policy) they care about.

Experience American culture through little league to professional sports games, baking apple pies, connecting in person in 3rd spaces outside where you live or work, singing together. Incorporate the world while you're at it and learn about cultural holidays, try new foods, read global stories, explore maps and globes, listen to world music, visit cultural museums or festivals, and talk with people in your own community.

Learn together about anything and everything. Look it up and talk about it! Best use of that screen.

Prioritize Family Time

Sharing meals decreases stress, so try to have your meals all together and encourage thoughtful and hopeful discussion. Have family meetings and discuss your wellbeing and what needs to get done. Dedicate a little down time together sometimes, where your kids know you're right where you want to be.

Take Care of The Home Team

Understand that food and nutrition hold the key to how your body grows, builds, and functions. Drink water, eat the rainbow, read the labels. Involve your kids in cooking and make it fun with music or pretending to be restaurant staff.

Get up and move! Dance with your kids, walk, jump rope, stretch, kickbox, yoga, sit-ups and pushups 'nem, gym time, YouTube videos, stairs... get those heart rates up! Good habits and discipline up! Mood, energy, and cognitive function up! Life expectancy up!

Keep your soul lifted through prayer, meditation, and rest. Try to bring peace into yourself. Be the peace around you and reject the chaos. Get enough sleep to reset and replenish your body and your mind. Make time regularly for an activity you enjoy. Spend time outdoors around trees and in nature whenever you can. Stay in community - where you're valued and comfortable.

Hope and Faith: Daily Vitamins for Democracy

Hope is the belief the future will be better than today, and you play a role in making our future possible. Faith is similar to hope, but faith is in the present, not the future. Faith in God, the divine energy with us always, helps us to be thankful. It makes us smile and shows God's countenance to those who need to feel it, too.

Teach your kids to pray at bedtime, when washing their hands, anytime. Our family prays together before meals. Each night someone volunteers. It can be as simple as "Thank you, God", or a rhyme (God is good. God is great. Thank you for the food on my plate), or prayer for specific people or problems, but the theme is gratitude to God for food, family, and life.

That gratitude helps us have faith in other things we can't see. We see that faith in God and faith in justice are cousins. That helping others is holy. That protecting the vulnerable is American.

PART FOUR

What We Can Do as a Community

Engage Your Community Reps

Have your children write letters to their Senators and Representatives. It doesn't have to be long. It can just be a statement of what their concern is, what policy they want the rep to address about it, and an appreciation for representing them. And parents can call the reps, local on up and tell them where you stand on an issue and why you care. Ask them how they'll vote on the issue. Ask about expanding parks and rec classes. Ask about their votes to support community funding vs. votes for billionaire tax cuts.

Rep Your Engaging Community

Those 3rd spaces are great avenues for organizing learning and action outings. Get with your church, school/PTA, neighborhood, social groups, clubs, etc. to go to a city council meeting or a school board meeting. See real debates and decision-making in action. Review the agenda in advance to understand the key issues, perhaps petition to speak on one.

Put the UNITY in Community

This one is for us and them. Community knowledge breeds community action, so get in the know and talk about what's going on with your friends and social groups! Tell the stories of victories. Party with a cause.

Determine how to use your economic power and what businesses and organizations you'll support that align with your values. Use your money and time wisely. In organizing action, there are economic resources and moral resources. Economic resources deplete with use, but moral resources grow. Grow!

What We Need from our Leaders

Blitz us with that good legislative language prepared for use in different jurisdictions that addresses our common interests and the common good. A breakdown of which offices need a candidate to get specific outcomes. Strategies on how to combine our collective power. I'd love a vetted list of corporations who advocate for good, so we can support and build together.

Aunt America Is Counting on Us

She's bruised but not broken, and she can be better than ever! She needs us to raise better citizens so the whole American family knows how to love her and keep her strong.

So, teach them. Talk and tell the stories, the truth. Let them lead in saying grace. And if they pray for mommy's job? Smile and know they're paying attention. They care. They have the tools to do something about it. Know Aunt America still has a shot with them on the team...and they have a shot at the Dream.

Visionary Author | Deitra Wynn Scott

Deitra Wynn Scott is a community health nurse with over 20 years of experience designing, implementing, and advocating for programs and policies that empower families and communities. Having lived in rural, suburban, and urban America, she brings a unique lens to the forces that divide, and can unite, us. Deitra and her husband, Woody, met at Georgetown University and now share four amazing children who they are raising to be thoughtful, engaged citizens. Deitra is excited to share practical strategies and heartfelt wisdom to help parents navigate today's complex political landscape and guide their children toward active, compassionate citizenship - rooted in love for self, community, country, God, and all God's children. Visit her website www.PA4Real.com for resources, links, details, and pursuits related to information discussed in this guide.

NOTES

NOTES

NOTES

Transform, Transcend, and Flourish: The Joy of Resilience

Dr. Susan Dandridge

BAM!

*S*creaming! (*In my head*) *I have been hit. Where am I? Where is my car headed? Concentrate. Keep your head in a crisis. What do you need to do? Glass is still flying, and the car is still moving fast. Glass everywhere. My hair, my skin, my eyes. Oh My God!! My EYES! Close your eyes. No, don't close your eyes! Keep your wits about you. Am I on the road? Will other cars or trucks or semis hit me? Will I hit a tree? I should brake. My leg, I can't move my right leg. Try with your left foot. Can't, it's on fire! Is the car on fire?! No, it's not. Neither the car nor my leg. Phew! Make it move. Oh no, the brakes are out! The passenger side of the car is practically gone. OMG This might be it.*

Well, guess what?! I'm still here!

Following the accident, I had to recover from three fractured vertebrae, both sides of my pelvis fractured, severely sprained ankles, internal injuries, cuts, and burns (my legs *were* actually burned from the release of the hot air bags). Miraculously, there was no damage to my eyes from the glass. Thank you, God.

Initially, I found the most difficult task was telling my four children about the accident and my injuries. I'm the mom. I'm supposed to be the one taking care of everything and everyone. I bear the brunt of the worries for the family. I know if I tell them, they will worry. Having my two young adults, one collegian, and one high schooler worry about me made me more anxious than the road to recovery I was facing. Therefore, I did not tell them the extent of my injuries. I did not tell them the doctors *hoped* I would walk again, but could not say it with certainty. They did say I would probably walk again, albeit with a limp, a cane, or even a walker. So began my convalescence.

What I didn't consider was that I was on my own. I was dating someone, but I was not married, and he lived over an hour away. My family doesn't live in the same state and my friends were all busy with their lives. And to top it all off, we were in the throes of the more virulent variant of COVID-19, so not only were people busy, but they were also avoidant about interacting with others and traveling. Fortunately, my cousin came to get me situated and friends dropped off care packages from time to time. For the activities of daily living, I had to turn to my 15-year-old, who was the only one in the house with me. After my cousin Melissa left to go back to North Carolina, internally I was a mess, but I tried not to show it. Taylor turned to me and said, "It's OK, Mommy. I'm here."

I spent 10 weeks at home and the first seven of those in bed. And we managed. She stayed by my side as I struggled with the walker to the bathroom, prepared my food and brought it to me before she left for school and when she came home from practice in the evenings. We spent the evenings watching shows together and playing games. She would send me cheerful notes during the day, and every day remind me of the things to smile about. "Look Mom, your sausage toes aren't swollen anymore!"

Ironically, I had been thinking about writing a book about resilience since "back in the day". I had always put it off thinking, *what credibility do I have about resilience?* Divorce had been the most difficult experience in my life, and I didn't think that was any big deal. But now here I was, putting into practice all the coping strategies I had been teaching others. I finally had my lived experience; not only did it transform me, but I came out stronger, kinder, and more joyful. Here are my top three coping strategies:

1. **Gratitude**—I found a lot to be grateful for in the situation. I did not have any eye damage, despite having tiny glass shards in my eyes. I healed quickly, and with physical therapy was able to walk again, without a limp or any device needed! In fact, by my birthday five months after the accident, I was able to dance and lead the dance train around the party. I started a gratitude journal. I wrote about the people and things for which I was thankful and still continue it to this day. It helps me look for the positive in each day.

2. **Connection**—I had the opportunity to really connect with my youngest child in a way that most parents, including myself, do not connect with their children. I was able to be vulnerable and let her take care of me. I was no longer the mom making orders about cleaning, washing dishes, saying go to bed, or anything. I had to let go and let her handle her own affairs. That freed me to just enjoy her company, ask about her life, watch shows together, and laugh with one another. I was also able to

connect with others via social media and virtually. We had extended family video chats for the first time ever. I was able to slow down from my busy life and enjoy deepening relationships.

3. **Mindfulness**—It would have been easy to replay the accident in my head over and over. Or detail it again and again to everyone who asked, "What happened?" I could have also dwelled on my injuries; the ugliness of my scars and lack of functioning of my limbs and wonder if I would ever walk normally again. Yet instead, I focused on the present. I did deep breathing, grounding exercises, guided imagery, and progressive relaxation. I kept reminding myself of the beauty in the moment. I did not allow myself to replay the scene or think of the "what ifs."

I thank God for my healing. I am thankful for my psychology background in helping me create joy while navigating this difficult experience and strengthening my ability to bounce back from adversity. I am also thankful that my daughter saw me through it, ultimately developing her own sense of fortitude and positivity. We are resilient!

Visionary Author | Dr. Susan Dandridge

Dr. Susan Dandridge is a Licensed Clinical Psychologist, dynamic consultant, sought-after speaker, and skilled trainer. She is the President and Founder of The Dragonfly Group: Coaching, Consulting, and Counseling, LLC and a graduate of Yale and Virginia Commonwealth Universities. As a dedicated mom of four plus four more, and a resilience expert, she is passionate about empowering individuals and organizations to thrive through change. She and her husband, Dr. Shawn Dandridge, love to travel the world, visiting museums and attending concerts along the way.

NOTES

NOTES

NOTES

You Never Know

Dr. Shawn Dandridge

I desire that by sharing a little of what I have lived and heard from others, I may be able to help someone. I am a father/bonus parent of eight children, ranging in age from their 30s to their teenage years. This is my second go-round of being involved with a blended family. Blood relationships or relational roles to the children are not the sole focus of this writing. I want to remind anyone who will read this, as I have had to remind myself, that you never know.

Raising children correctly is one of a parent's most important and meaningful endeavors. Helping to shape a child's life and give a foundation for their character while influencing their future relationships will impact the kind of adult they become. When a parent focuses on instilling values, such as honesty, kindness, responsibility, and resilience, they are aiming to prepare their child for the complexities of life that are sure to come.

Proper upbringing usually leads to a self-sufficient, respectful, and empathic adult. As a pastor, I must add that teaching children to unlock their faith and trust in God is essential to their success.

Structure and creating boundaries they can appreciate and duplicate later in life will also be key to avoiding unnecessary pitfalls, but you never know.

Despite parents' best efforts, raising children correctly does not guarantee they will follow the path laid before them. It also does not guarantee they will remain close, uphold the same values, or believe in God as they age. We are all inherently complex, and the sooner we embrace that truth, the sooner we can brace ourselves for some things we may never understand.

I was recently asked, "When did you give your youngest child a cell phone?" My truthful answer was age seven. At the time, I thought how cute it would be to send a text periodically to my kid and for me to get a response. I had zero consideration for how the phone would really be used. Fast forward to today, I understand the reality of Snapchat, Instagram, Facebook, Google, YouTube, TikTok, and other platforms. These online avenues are in addition to the influences of peers, books, TV, and their internal struggles. These influences can lead them to question or reject parental teaching. They may encounter situations that challenge their beliefs or push them toward behaviors that do not reflect the values they were raised with.

The old adage of "if I knew then what I know now" came into play many years ago; I would have waited many years before giving any kid a phone and placed restrictions on it. Two of those restrictions would have been time limits and blocking certain sites.

While questioning and experimenting are natural processes in human development, how people respond and react will impact how they forge their identity. Life's circumstances can create distance between parents and their children. This can happen when a child moves away for college or a job. Children may feel misunderstood or judged by their parents, especially if they have decided to have different values from those taught at home.

No matter how well a child is raised, they have free will. There is a good chance they will stray from the path their parents envisioned, and some will completely go off course and create their own pathway. This can be a painful and stressful time. You never know.

I vividly recall getting pushback from one of my children once they got their first job. I believe in working and budgeting, but my teenager at the time did not want to budget. They wanted to use their money to buy video games and fast food. They did not want to hear me telling them to stop blowing their paycheck each week. While they always heard me share with them to know the price of everything and to appreciate value, they did not practice this. Even as adults, they have not grasped the concept of budgeting.

I have said quite a bit that could be perceived as negative, yet it is a possible reality. Despite these challenges, I want you to remember that your efforts are necessary and valuable. Proper upbringing plants the seeds that can influence your child for a lifetime. Even if the child strays or follows your blueprint, the correct early foundation can be a source of strength and possible reconciliation.

What is most important is the hope that the values and love shared in those formative years, and much later, will always resonate with them. Sometimes the journey involves letting go, giving space, and maybe even offering forgiveness.

Do all you can to leave a legacy of love and understanding while remaining that safe place for them. I hold on to the fact that I taught them things that can improve their lives and are invaluable. I shared things I learned from my parents and gained from experience. What kind of parents would we be if we did not attempt to give our children the best of who we are and attempt to steer them from possible pitfalls? Try as we might to see that they develop and grow to be the best version of themselves and achieve high levels of greatness, you never know. I want to implore you not to let not knowing stop you from loving them for who they are or who they will become. At the end of the day, you will always be mom/dad.

Do not be afraid to seek counseling. Prayer is always available, and books can encourage you or add insight. In the meantime, I will be praying for a loving, respectful, and close relationship between parents and their children. We need strong, united, caring, and productive families to make this world a better place.

My wife and I have similarities in our family structure, and we have plenty of education and experience to assist those who desire help. We created the Dragonfly Consulting Group, and under that umbrella, we do many things, including workshops on healthy relationships.

Visionary Author | Dr. Shawn Dandridge

Dr. Shawn Dandridge is married to an amazing woman and the father/bonus parent of eight children. He has a doctorate and multiple master's degrees. He has a passion for lifelong learning and loves reading, attending concerts, and exploring new places. Professionally, he serves as a pastor, sales representative, and adjunct professor. Balancing faith, business, and education are important to him, and his trademark in life is #laughnpraydaily. Dedicated to positively impacting his community and beyond, Dr. Dandridge enjoys connecting with others and embracing diverse experiences.

NOTES

NOTES

NOTES

How to Be the Parent Your LGBTQIA+ Child Needs When Coming Out

Dr. Demetria Bates

Dear Parents,

Take a deep breath and imagine your child feeling isolated, sad, and alone. A child who does not feel safe enough to share how they truly feel. A child that is afraid to disappoint you, upset you, or lose your love. A child who looks elsewhere for belonging and understanding because they do not feel accepted, confident, or secure enough to come to you.

Now, imagine the courage it takes for that same child to approach you years later and say, *"I'm gay."* This moment is commonly referred to as "coming out of the closet." It is a declaration of truth after years of secrecy, fear, and internal questioning of *"will my parents still love me if I tell them?"* LGBTQIA+ individuals raised in religious or conservative homes often face judgment, bible thumping, and harsh opinions.

For years, I rehearsed the words in my head. I cried in silence, weighed down by the emotional burden of hiding—which only deepened my depression and anxiety. I will never forget the moment I came out to my father. After I said the words, "I'm gay," there was a heavy silence. My heart was pounding so loud I could hear it echoing in my ears. I braced for rejection. Instead, he said, *"Okay, well thank you for telling me—but does your mama know?"*

It was not a big speech, but it gave me hope.

This is just a brief glimpse into my coming out story. Honestly, that moment did not erase the fear or uncertainty I had carried for years, but it reminded me that love can break through discomfort—and that was enough to keep the door open.

I did not need my parents to have all the right words. I did not need them to instantly understand everything.

What I needed was simple: to be seen, heard, and—above all else—loved without judgment.

Parents, your first response matters. Your words, your facial expressions, your body language, each one sends a message. Even if you feel surprised, confused, or scared, the most important thing you can convey is that your love is unwavering.

It is okay to say, *"I don't fully understand"* or *"I need time to process this."* Just make sure you end the conversation with: **"I love you, and I'm here."**

Parents please do not let your child feel like they are a disappointment or a burden because that response can cause deep emotional harm which could cause your child to unalive themselves.

To be honest, parents often feel like they have failed parenting by asking, *"Where did I go wrong?"* I'm here to tell you that you did not do anything wrong, but you are grieving the future you once imagined for your child, or you may be afraid of the difficulties they'll face in a world that is not always kind to LGBTQIA+ individuals.

Your willingness to process this moment will shape how you show up for your child during one of the most vulnerable times in their life. There is **no greater gift** you can give your child than unconditional love. Your acceptance can be the difference between them merely surviving or living authentically.

The world can be harsh. People will judge, misunderstand, and at times, hurt them but do not let your love be one more thing they have to fear. Let your love be their shield and comfort.

If you are unsure where to begin, I have included six self-reflection questions and included a bonus of several resources to help guide you through this process.

With love and hope,

Dr. Demetria Bates, DNP, FNP-BC
A once-closeted child, now living in truth.

Self- Reflection Questions

Take a quiet moment to reflect on these questions. Be honest, be gentle with yourself, and keep your heart open.

1. Am I willing to do the internal work necessary to grow and show up for my child, even if it is uncomfortable?
2. What messages did I receive growing up about sexuality and gender? How might those messages be influencing my current reactions?
3. Am I holding on to any expectations or assumptions about my child's future that I now realize are based on my own fears or beliefs?
4. Have I taken time to learn more about my child's identity, or am I relying only on what I already know (or assume)?
5. What worries me most about my child being part of the LGBTQIA+ community? Are these worries based on facts, fears, or stereotypes?
6. What small step can I take this week to show my child that I am committed to loving and supporting them as they are?

BONUS: 5 Trusted Resources for Parents of LGBTQIA+ Children

1. PFLAG

- www.pflag.org
- Founded in 1973, PFLAG is the first and largest organization for LGBTQIA+ people, their parents, and

families. Offers nationwide support groups, educational materials, and advocacy training.

2. The Trevor Project – Parent & Caregiver Resources

- https://www.thetrevorproject.org/
- A leading crisis and suicide prevention organization for LGBTQIA+ youth. Their parent resources include guides on coming out, mental health, and building affirming relationships.

3. Gender Spectrum

- www.genderspectrum.org
- Offers research-informed resources to help parents understand gender diversity and support their child through developmentally appropriate frameworks.

4. Family Acceptance Project (San Francisco State University)

- https://familyproject.sfsu.edu/
- An evidence-based research initiative that provides tools and guidance to help families reduce rejection and improve outcomes for LGBTQIA+ youth.

5. Human Rights Campaign – Parents & Families Resources

- www.hrc.org
- The HRC's resources for parents include educational tools, FAQs, coming out guides, and ways to create inclusive family spaces based on national policy and research.

Visionary Author | Dr. Demetria Bates

Dr. Demetria Bates is a Board-Certified Family Nurse Practitioner and founder of Bates Virtual Health & Consultants, LLC, a virtual Cannabis consulting practice offering medical card services and education to Virginia residents. She earned her Doctorate in Nursing Practice from Liberty University and specializes in Cannabis medicine and weight management. With over 15 years of nursing experience, she is also a Certified Cannabis Educator and Health Coach. She is an Army veteran, LGBTQIA+ advocate, wife, and mom. Dr. Bates is dedicated to empowering clients toward better health and advancing change in healthcare through education and advocacy.

NOTES

NOTES

NOTES

The Power of T.A.L.K.
Dr. Shawnrell Blackwell

How the hell can I write about parenting when my own son doesn't even TALK to me?

T hat question haunted me. It looped in my mind like a song I couldn't turn off. How do you write about parenting when what you're trying to write about feels broken?

At first, I thought I had to say no. I thought I had to wait until things were repaired. But the more I sat with it, the more I realized this is the story. The silence is part of the story. The struggle, the shame, the questions—they are the story.

That question almost silenced me. But this chapter isn't about a perfect picture of parenthood. It's about the truth. It's about what happens when we get it wrong—and what we do next. Maybe the most important parenting lessons come after the mistakes.

The truth is, I messed up. This reminds me of how I felt as an adult when I told my parents I was marrying a woman. It was a moment soaked in truth and trembling with hope—hope that they would see me, hold me, and love me, even when they didn't fully understand.

My mother didn't celebrate. She didn't say "I'm happy for you" or "I'm proud." What she gave me was silence wrapped in discomfort. But she showed up. She came to the wedding. She took pictures. She made awkward small talk with people she knew, trying to explain how her daughter was marrying a woman. And over time, she kept showing up—until the awkwardness softened into something that resembled love. Not perfect love, but chosen love.

My father made a different choice. He stayed home. His absence echoed through every toast, every hug, every dance. That absence stung in ways that still live in my bones. But it also taught me one of the deepest parenting lessons of all: presence matters—even when your child is grown. We don't stop needing our parents just because we age out of their house. We don't stop craving their approval, their support, their love. Sometimes, we need it even more than adults—when life gets more complicated, when identity becomes clearer, when healing feels overdue.

Even when it's imperfect. Even when it's uneasy. Just being there speaks volumes even when you don't have the right words. I was a grown woman—strong, accomplished, and deeply in love— standing at the altar, still wishing my father had walked through that door. I wasn't looking for perfection. I was hoping for effort. I didn't need him to understand everything about my life or agree with every choice—I just needed him to show up.

He didn't.

And now, I wonder if I've done the same to my own child.

Have I become my father?

Like my mother, I became a single parent. I hustled. I protected. I provided. But I didn't always give my son what I needed from my parents: a safe space to be fully, freely himself.

I talked at him, not with him. I corrected, disciplined, provided— but I didn't always listen. I reacted instead of responding. I showed love through structure and provision, but I missed something: I didn't listen enough.

Now he's grown. And the silence between us is louder than ever. It's the result of missed moments, avoided conversations, and love that was implied—but not always expressed.

We live in the ache of unspoken words. But that silence also teaches.

That's why I created T.A.L.K.—Tolerance, Acceptance, Love, and Kindness. Not just a framework, but a lifeline. A reminder to slow down, listen deeper, love harder, and hold space for our children to show up as their whole selves.

T—Tolerance

Tolerance means pausing long enough to say, "I don't get it—but I'm staying."

For me, that began at home. To my mother, *appearance was everything*. I know it wasn't easy for her. She made awkward small talk with people she knew, trying to explain how her daughter was marrying a woman. I can only imagine the mental gymnastics it took for her to reconcile her faith, her upbringing, and her love for me in public spaces where judgment felt ever-present.

But she tolerated it. Even if she didn't fully understand, she stood beside me.

Did I forget my son had to tolerate being the son of a Black queer woman? Trying to define manhood while I was still figuring myself out?

Even knowing what intolerance feels like, I didn't always tolerate his truth—his anger, his quiet, his questions. I missed chances to hold space when he needed feeling, not fixing.

Remember This:

Tolerance is not silence — it is the choice to listen, to stay, and to try even when understanding doesn't come easily.

Action Step:

Practice sitting with discomfort. The next time a loved one shares something that challenges your beliefs, don't react — just listen. Breathe. Let curiosity lead instead of judgment.

A—Acceptance

Acceptance says, "I see you—not who I hoped you'd be, but who you are—and I'm not leaving."

My mother didn't accept me right away. But she stayed long enough to learn how. She asked hard questions. She talked to other gay people at her job. She made mistakes. And eventually, she celebrated the love I built with my wife—not just tolerated it.

That kind of acceptance changed me. It healed old wounds I didn't know I still carried.

As parents, we don't get to write our child's story. But we do get to be faithful readers of it, even when the plot twists scare us.

My son had been an incredible athlete and student. But by senior year, he began making choices I didn't agree with. And my responses? Sharp, cold, and judgmental.

I believed I was modeling greatness: I bought my first home at 23. I earned my Ph.D. from Virginia Tech. I climbed the ranks as an educator and a leader. I thought he'd naturally follow suit. So, when he dropped out of college in his first semester and couldn't keep a steady job, I couldn't understand.

The math wasn't mathing.

I believed he'd follow my path—but maybe his journey wasn't a failure. Maybe I failed to accept it.

Remember This:
Acceptance isn't agreement — it's surrendering the need to change someone to love them.

Action Step:
Name something about your child or loved one you've struggled to accept. Say it aloud. Then follow it with: *"And I love them fully, even here."*

L—Love

There's the kind of love that pays bills—and the kind that says, "What's going on in that heart of yours?"

I was good at the first. I struggled with the second.

Love isn't just about giving—it's about showing up with empathy, even when it's hard.

Eventually, my son enrolled in the Air Force. He left home with no debt, a paid-for car. I thought that was enough. I thought I had "arrived" as a parent.

But then he spiraled into debt and failed relationships. And in my frustration, I withdrew. I stopped supporting him financially. I stopped showing him love in the way he needed.

I became ashamed, embarrassed by his choices. In that shame, I mirrored exactly what I hated receiving from others—conditional love.

That's what I had once received—and what I was now giving.

But I've learned: real love doesn't require full understanding. It just requires full presence.

Remember This:
Love is not just a feeling. It's a verb. It shows up in late-night calls, quiet hugs, and the hard conversations we don't want to have but choose, anyway.

Action Step:
Write a note (text, letter, or journal) to your child, partner, or even yourself, expressing love without condition — no matter the choices made, the distance, or the past.

K—Kindness

Kindness is where healing begins. It's the soft landing after a hard truth. It's the *"I see you"* after the *"I'm sorry."*

When my son was becoming—figuring himself out—I met him with pressure, not patience. I tried to be tough to fill his father's absence. I forgot that kindness is not weakness—it's strength.

I still try to mend our relationship. I call and text, but it's not the same.

What I would give for a hug. To lay his head on my chest like I did when he was a baby. To remind him that no matter what—my love for him has never wavered. Even when I didn't have the right words. Even when I didn't know how to show it.

Kindness means understanding we are all just doing the best we can, often with broken tools. It means giving grace, even when it's not returned. And above all, it means trying again tomorrow. So tomorrow, I will text and call again.

Remember This:
Kindness is not weakness — it is the most radical form of strength. It heals. It builds bridges. And it begins with how we speak to ourselves.

Action Step:
Today, give yourself kindness first. Replace one harsh inner thought with a gentle one. Then, pass that energy on to someone else: a smile, a compliment, or a moment of grace.

So, what's the takeaway here?

This chapter isn't for perfect parents. It's for those who are tired, honest, and still trying, for those who want to break cycles, not repeat them.

Here's what I know now:

- **Your child doesn't need a perfect parent. They need an honest one.** When you mess up, own it. When you're confused, say so. Let your child see your humanity.

- **It's never too late to reconnect.** Silence can be deafening—but it's not final. Keep reaching. Keep texting. Keep showing up.

- **Your identity doesn't disqualify you from giving wisdom.** As a queer Black woman, I've had to navigate spaces that didn't see me. But I've also built bridges. My identity is not an obstacle—it's a lens. A gift. A testimony of what love can endure and what healing can look like.

- **Forgive yourself for what you didn't know then.** We can't go back, but we can begin again. And again. And again.

Ironically, I was always labeled as "talkative" in school—but over time, I learned it's not just **what** you say, it's **how** you say it. Parents, mind how you **T.A.L.K.**—because your tone, your timing, and your truth can either open hearts or close doors.

I'm still learning how to **T.A.L.K.** I'm still unlearning old ways of parenting. I'm still showing up—even when the door isn't open—because that's what love does.

If you've messed up like I have—if your child isn't talking to you, if you feel like you've failed them—just know this doesn't have to be the end of the story.

You still have time.

Not to be perfect. Just to be present.

And that's where the power of **T.A.L.K.** lives.

Reflection Prompt: Who Do You Need to T.A.L.K. To?

Take a moment and sit with these questions:

- Who in your life have you only tolerated, but never truly accepted?
- Where have you shown up physically but failed to be emotionally present?
- When was the last time you responded to a loved one with unconditional love rather than unmet expectations?
- Have you offered kindness to others in the same measure that you offer it to yourself?

Parent. Child. Friend. Partner. You.

Maybe the conversation you need to have is overdue. Maybe the healing starts with a simple "I'm sorry," or "I didn't know how," or "I'm still learning."

T.A.L.K. is more than a chapter—it's an invitation to reconnect with the parts of ourselves and others that we've silenced.

So—who do you need to talk to?

Reflective Verses:

The Poetry That Holds My Truths

Since I was very young, writing has been one of the ways I've learned to breathe through the hardest moments—one of my many coping tools (but that's a whole other book, lol). What began as journaling and poetry to make sense of the world eventually led me to major in English and become a teacher. I wanted to help others discover what I had found: the power of writing to heal, to testify, to remember.

Poetry, especially, became a sacred space. A place where I could speak when speaking felt too hard. I still hold on to many of the poems I wrote in high school and college—tucked away like love letters to myself. One day, I'll share them all with the world.

But today, I share *Jalen*, a ballad I wrote for my son in 1999 for a college class assignment. I titled the poem "Jalen, a reflection of a cesarean birth, love, and everything I carried as a 20-year-old Black woman becoming a mother."

Jalen by Dr. Shawnrell Blackwell

"Tell me the story again, Mom."
"Okay, my only son."

"As my flowering skin blossomed
Upon your arrival.
I watched your limbs root and branch out,
The signs of survival.
A seed growing like a wild rose
In a forest wrapped in love.
Calmly, water broke the still —
Trickling waterfalls from above.

Then rapids rose and raged against
The calm, the line of life.
The resurrection of new breath
Cut through me like a knife.
As my womanhood was widened —
A sacred wound, I cried.
You clung to me so fiercely, then,
You almost, nearly died.

Now I bear the scars of giving you life
For all the world to see.

The Power of T.A.L.K.

Thank you, Heavenly Father, for
Giving my son to me.
My precious angel to the world.
My joy, my beating heart.
I will do it all over again.
I can't imagine us apart."

Visionary Author | Dr. Shawnrell Blackwell

Dr. Shawnrell Blackwell, widely known as *Dr. B*, is a force of nature—where purpose, power, and passion collide. With over 20 years in educational leadership, she has dedicated her life to moving people—mind, body, and spirit. As a certified fitness instructor, realtor, author, and spoken word artist, Dr. B lives boldly at the intersection of wellness, women's empowerment, and community service.

Her signature T.A.L.K. method transforms everyday conversations into intentional, healing dialogue, and her voice, whether in classrooms or on stages, has inspired thousands to rise and own their truth. From serving on the Virginia Governor's Council on Women to performing her debut spoken word single, Sis, Breathe, Dr. B embodies a mission bigger than herself: helping women move with purpose and build a legacy.

"The Power of TALK" isn't just a concept—it's a catalyst. A bold invitation to speak life, lead with intention, and transform how we connect. **Now, are you ready to TALK about it?**

NOTES

NOTES

NOTES